THE
GOLIATH
CODE

A BIBLICAL BATTLE PLAN
FOR DEFEATING ANY GIANT

BLAKE WATKINS

THE GOLIATH CODE
A BIBLICAL BATTLE PLAN
UNDERSTANDING THIS STUDY GUIDE

This is an in-depth study into The GOLIATH CODE, a Biblical Battle Plan for spiritual warfare, based on 1 Samuel 17. It consists of thirteen sessions, including an introduction (or prologue), the eleven chapters in the book, and an epilogue.

Each study session should include the following:

Prayer—Begin by asking the Lord to lead and guide the study, and to open each participant's heart to His presence and teaching.

Review—Review the acrostic GOLIATH CODE (found in the introduction/Prologue), and the Strategy Summary and Key Point from the previous session (if any). Discuss whether and how this study has begun to affect the lives of the participants.

Key Verses—Each session, other than the Prologue and Epilogue, has four or five key Bible verses to complete by filling in the blanks. To get the most benefit, you can also choose to memorize one or all of them. Note: Unless otherwise stated, all quotations are from the New King James Version.

Video Streaming—Each session includes a video-streaming episode based on the corresponding chapter in The GOLIATH CODE. Except for the Prologue and Epilogue, each video consists of two parts: History and Strategy.

Use the printed Study Guide to follow along with each video.

The History section begins with the biblical text from 1 Samuel 17, and includes space for notes along with a list of the scriptures referenced in the video.

The Strategy section explains the Key word, from the acrostic GOLIATH CODE, corresponding to that session, and includes space for notes along with a list of the scriptures referenced in the video.

The Study Guide for each session, except for the Prologue and Epilogue, also includes a page listing the Key Word, Key Verses (see above), Key Terms, and Key Point for future reference.

Think About It—Talk About It: Each session includes several questions designed to encourage open and honest discussion, and to aid in understanding the biblical concepts taught in each session.

Closing Word – Summarize each session by reviewing the Key Point and the acrostic GOLIATH CODE. Challenge the participants to memorize some of the Key Verses and begin to apply what they have learned in the spiritual battles they face that week. Close with Prayer.

Also included in this Study Guide are the following appendices:

Labels God Gives Us (Who We Are In Christ)

How To Become a New Creation (The ABCs of Salvation)

THE GOLIATH CODE
A BIBLICAL BATTLE PLAN
INTRODUCTION

Summary: We each fight battles like this one, facing enemies bigger, stronger, and more experienced than us. We have adversaries who seem like giants—giants who hate us and try to stop us from doing what God has created, called, and empowered us to do. These giants want to drag us back into bondage and destroy us.

Beneath the surface of this familiar story is a "secret code" of vital information we can use to win our spiritual battles with the giants who come against us. I call it *The Goliath Code*.

The foundation of *The Goliath Code* is an unshakable faith in the absolute truth of God's Word, the Bible.

I agree with Augustine when he said, "If you believe what you like in the Bible, and don't believe what you don't like in the Bible, then it is not the Bible you believe—it is yourself." We must let the Scriptures judge us, rather than us judge them.

David's victory vividly illustrates how we, too, can conquer our giants.

To help you remember and apply this biblical strategy to your battles, I created the acrostic GOLIATH CODE. Each letter in this mnemonic corresponds to a key word that heads each chapter and summarizes the main theme of the part of the battle plan contained in the passage.

G: Geography—Understand the Geography

O: Opponent—Recognize Your Opponent

L: Labels—Use the Right Labels

I: Intrepid—Be Intrepid

A: Aim—Aim to Please God

T: Truth—Speak the Truth

H: Hardware—Use the Right Hardware

C: Confess—Confess the Lord

O: Overcome—Overcome!

D: Demonstrate—Demonstrate Your Faith

E: Endure—Endure to the End

My prayer is that you, if you are a child of the King, will glory in the search for the amazing truths concealed in this story and that you will allow God's Word to pierce into you, pruning your thoughts and beliefs.

Most importantly, if you have not yet decided to accept Jesus as your Lord, then I pray you will meet Him through this study and choose to place your trust in Him. Then—and only then—you, like David, can run to the battle in confidence and be more than a conqueror through Him who loves us.

References:

Revelation 12:1   John 17:17

Proverbs 25:2   Psalm 119:105   Hebrews 4:12

KEY WORDS

Fill in the blanks with the key words: (HINT: See previous page for answers.)

The GOLIATH CODE

G: Understand the _____

O: Recognize Your _____

L: Use the Right _____

I: Be _____

A: _____ to Please God

T: Speak the _____

H: Use the Right _____

C: _____ the Lord

O: _____!

D: _____ Your Faith

E: _____ to the End

THINK ABOUT IT—TALK ABOUT IT

1. What do you hope to learn from this study?

_____

_____

_____

2. What struggles are you facing now that you believe are spiritual battles?

_____

_____

_____

3. Do you believe that the Bible is the word of God? Have you found it to be the truth?

_____

_____

_____

_____

THE GOLIATH CODE
A BIBLICAL BATTLE PLAN
SESSION 1: GEOGRAPHY

HISTORY: THE BATTLEFIELD

Text: 1 Samuel 17:1-3

"Now the Philistines gathered their armies together to battle, and were gathered at Sochoh, which belongs to Judah; they encamped between Sochoh and Azekah, in Ephes Dammim. And Saul and the men of Israel were gathered together, and they encamped in the Valley of Elah, and drew up in battle array against the Philistines. The Philistines stood on a mountain on one side, and Israel stood on a mountain on the other side, with a valley between them."

References:

Numbers 13:27   Job 1:10
Matthew 21:33   Psalm 139:5   Exodus 12:23

STRATEGY: G–GEOGRAPHY–UNDERSTAND THE GEOGRAPHY.

Summary: We are at war. Our demonic adversary is seeking to destroy us. But his forces are wedged between a hedge and a fence and can never cross the boundary of Jesus' blood. God's people, on the other hand, are sheltered in Christ, the Ram—the position of strength.

References:

Isaiah 14:13-14
Ezekiel 28:16b-17
Revelation 12:3-4a
Revelation 12:7-9
Revelation 12:12

1 Peter 5:8-9
2 Timothy 3:12
John 10:28-29
Revelation 1:5-6
Psalm 61:3

Psalm 143:9
Luke 22:31-32
Matthew 10:28-31
Matthew 16:18

KEY WORD: GEOGRAPHY

Key Verses: (fill in the blanks)

"Be sober, be vigilant; because your _____ the devil walks about like a roaring lion, seeking whom he may devour. _____ him, steadfast in the faith, knowing that the same sufferings are experienced by your brotherhood in the world" (1 Peter 5:8-9).

"And I give them eternal life, and they shall never perish; neither shall anyone snatch them out of My hand. My Father, who has given them to Me, is greater than all; and no one is able to snatch them out of My Father's _____" (John 10:28-29).

"Now thanks be to God who always leads us in triumph ____ _____!" (2 Corinthians 2:14).

"For You have been a _____ for me, a strong tower from the enemy" (Psalm 61:3).

KEY TERMS:

Philistines: rolling; migrating

Azekah: Fence

Sochoh: Hedge

Ephes Dammim: Boundary of the Blood Drops

Selah: stop and think

El: God

Elah: Grace of God

Elyon: Most High

KEY POINT:

"Never forget where you are. If you are a Christian, the Bible says you are "in Christ." The New Testament uses the phrase more than eighty-five times, and it is the most common description of those who are saved (compared to only three instances for the word Christian)."

THINK ABOUT IT—TALK ABOUT IT

G: Understand the _____

1. Are you "in Christ"? If you cannot confidently say, "yes", then, the strategy in The Goliath Code will not work for you. But you can be if you want to be, so please stop right here and ask your group leader to explain God's free offer and how you can be in Christ.

2. What do you think it means to be "in Christ"?

3. Can you recall a verse that uses the phrase "in Christ", "in Him", "in God" or "in the Lord"?

4. How does knowing you are in Christ affect your confidence level?

5. How is Christ like a storm shelter?

_____

_____

6. What is the spiritual significance of the Hebrew name "Ephes Dammim"?

_____

_____

_____

_____

7. Since our enemy is spiritually hemmed in, can he hurt us?

_____

_____

_____

_____

8. Why do you suppose the Israelites did not understand the significance of the battlefield geography?

_____

_____

_____

_____

THE GOLIATH CODE
A BIBLICAL BATTLE PLAN
SESSION 2: OPPONENT

HISTORY: THE ADVERSARY

Text: 1 Samuel 17:4-11

"And a champion went out from the camp of the Philistines, named Goliath, from Gath, whose height was six cubits and a span. He had a bronze helmet on his head, and he was armed with a coat of mail, and the weight of the coat was five thousand shekels of bronze. And he had bronze armor on his legs and a bronze javelin between his shoulders. Now the staff of his spear was like a weaver's beam, and his iron spearhead weighed six hundred shekels; and a shield bearer went before him.

Then he stood and cried out to the armies of Israel, and said to them, 'Why have you come out to line up for battle? Am I not a Philistine, and you the servants of Saul? Choose a man for yourselves, and let him come down to me. If he is able to fight with me and kill me, then we will be your servants. But if I prevail against him and kill him, then you shall be our servants and serve us.' And the Philistine said, 'I defy the armies of Israel this day; give me a man, that we may fight together.' When Saul and all Israel heard these words of the Philistine, they were dismayed and greatly afraid" (1 Samuel 17:4-11).

References:

Genesis 6:4

Isaiah 14:12

Ecclesiastes 1:9-11

Numbers 13:31-33

1 Samuel 13:19-22

Deuteronomy 1:29-30

STRATEGY: O-OPPONENT-RECOGNIZE YOUR OPPONENT

Summary: A giant is anything bigger than you that stands in the way of completing the work God has given you to do. They threaten to either make you fall or force you back into bondage. Learn to recognize spiritual giants and the bondage they bring. Don't waste your time or ammunition fighting shield bearers.

References:

Hosea 4:11	2 Chronicles 20:15-17	
John 8:34-36	2 Corinthians 11:14	Galatians 5:1
2 Chronicles 20:3, 6, 12	Ephesians 6:12	

KEY WORD: OPPONENT

Key Verses: (fill in the blanks)

"There were _____ on the earth in those days, and also afterward, when the sons of God (Elohim) came in to the daughters of men (Adam) and they bore children to them. These were the mighty men of old, men of renown" (Genesis 6:4).

"And no wonder! For Satan Himself _____ himself into an angel of _____ " (2 Corinthians 11:14).

"For we do not wrestle against _____ and _____, but against principalities, against powers, against the rulers of the darkness of this age, against spiritual hosts of _____ in the heavenly places" (Ephesians 6:12).

"Stand fast therefore in the _____ by which Christ has made us free, and do not be entangled again with a yoke of _____ " (Galatians 5:1).

KEY TERMS:

Rapha: super strong; giant

Nephil: feller; giant

Gibbor: powerful bully or tyrant; giant

Adam: man

Nephilim: fallen ones; giants

Elohim: God

Champion: one who stands between two armies

Goliath: capture or place in bondage; splendor

Gath: winepress

KEY POINT:

"Giants still fight behind shield bearers today, just as Goliath did. However, a shield bearer is not a giant. A shield bearer is a human being who aids and defends the giant."

THINK ABOUT IT—TALK ABOUT IT

O: Recognize Your _____

1. List some giants you have had to face or are threatening you now.

2. How did these giants try to block you?

3. What bondage did they threaten to force you into?

4. Did you believe their threats? Did they succeed?

5. What are some ways you can recognize giants?

6. What does the name "Goliath" mean?

    _____

    _____

    _____

    _____

7. Why is it important to recognize your enemy?

    _____

    _____

    _____

    _____

8. Why is it important to understand that people are not giants?

    _____

    _____

    _____

    _____

9. Have you ever encountered a shield bearer for a giant?

    _____

    _____

    _____

    _____

THE GOLIATH CODE
A BIBLICAL BATTLE PLAN
SESSION 3: LABELS

HISTORY: THE HERO

Text: 1 Samuel 17:8b, 12-18

"Am I not a Philistine, and you the servants of Saul?" ...

Now David was the son of that Ephrathite of Bethlehem Judah, whose name was Jesse, and who had eight sons. And the man was old, advanced in years, in the days of Saul. The three oldest sons of Jesse had gone to follow Saul to the battle. The names of his three sons who went to the battle were Eliab the firstborn, next to him Abinadab, and the third Shammah. David was the youngest. And the three oldest followed Saul. But David occasionally went and returned from Saul to feed his father's sheep at Bethlehem. And the Philistine drew near and presented himself forty days, morning and evening.

Then Jesse said to his son David, 'Take now for your brothers an ephah of this dried grain and these ten loaves and run to your brothers at the camp. And carry these ten cheeses to the captain of their thousand, and see how your brothers fare, and bring back news of them'" (1 Samuel 17:8b,12-18).

References:

1 Samuel 16:18-21   Psalm 116:16

Colossians 3:20   Leviticus 25:55   1 Corinthians 1:10

STRATEGY: L–LABELS–USE THE RIGHT LABELS

Summary: Never accept the labels Satan, or the world, tries to stick on you. You are who God says you are—not what you do, or who you used to be. Learn to use the labels He gives you.

We tend to act like who we think we are.

References:

Mark 3:25
Romans 3:10
1 Corinthians 6:11
2 Corinthians 5:17
2 Timothy 3:5-7

John 8:26
John 12:49-50
John 14:24
John 17:17
Psalm 119:160

2 Corinthians 1:21-22
1 John 2:20
John 8:44

KEY WORD: LABELS

Key Verses: (fill in the blanks)

"And such _____ some of you. But you _____ washed, but you _____ sanctified, but you _____ justified in the name of the Lord Jesus and by the Spirit of our God" (1 Corinthians 6:11).

"O Lord, truly I am Your servant; I am Your servant, the son of Your maidservant; You have loosed my _____" (Psalm 116:16).

"Therefore, if anyone is in Christ, he is a _____ _____; old things have passed away; behold, all things have become _____" (2 Corinthians 5:17).

"Sanctify them by Your _____. Your _____ is truth" (John 17:17).

KEY TERMS:

Eliab: The God of Our Fathers

Abinadab: The Father of Liberals

Shammah: Stunned, or Stupefied

Carnal: fleshly, worldly

KEY POINT:

"The power of labels is that we believe them. We tend to believe we are who we and others say we are, especially when applied by people we respect or those who are supposed to love us. And it is human nature to act like who we think we are."

THINK ABOUT IT—TALK ABOUT IT

L: Use the Right _____

1. What labels have you worn in the past?

2. Is the saying, "If it walks like a duck and talks like a duck, it's a duck" true or false? Why?

3. What carnal labels are you tempted to accept for yourself or for others?

4. Why is it important for us to know what labels God gives us?

5. Why is it dangerous to use the wrong labels?

6. Review the list "Who We Are In Christ" in the Appendix. What is your favorite God-given label? Look up the Scripture reference for it.

_____

_____

_____

_____

7. How is it helpful for you to use this label?

_____

_____

_____

_____

8. Why is it so hard for us to accept that we are who God says we are?

_____

_____

_____

_____

9. How do we help others when we apply the right labels to them?

_____

_____

_____

_____

THE GOLIATH CODE
A BIBLICAL BATTLE PLAN
SESSION 4: INTREPID

HISTORY: THE TEST

Text: 1 Samuel 17:16, 19-27

"And the Philistine drew near and presented himself forty days, morning and evening . . .

Now Saul and they and all the men of Israel were in the Valley of Elah, fighting with the Philistines. So, David rose early in the morning, left the sheep with a keeper, and took the things and went as Jesse had commanded him. And he came to the camp as the army was going out to the fight and shouting for the battle. For Israel and the Philistines had drawn up in battle array, army against army. And David left his supplies in the hand of the supply keeper, ran to the army, and came and greeted his brothers.

Then as he talked with them, there was the champion, the Philistine of Gath, Goliath by name, coming up from the armies of the Philistines; and he spoke according to the same words. So, David heard them. And all the men of Israel, when they saw the man, fled from him and were dreadfully afraid. So, the men of Israel said, 'Have you seen this man who has come up? Surely, he has come up to defy Israel; and it shall be that the man who kills him the king will enrich with great riches, will give him his daughter, and give his father's house exemption from taxes in Israel.'

Then David spoke to the men who stood by him, saying, 'What shall be done for the man who kills this Philistine and takes away the reproach from Israel? For who is this uncircumcised Philistine, that he should defy the armies of the living God?' And the people answered him in this manner, saying, 'So shall it be done for the man who kills him'" (1 Samuel 17:16, 19-27).

References:

Deuteronomy 20:1-4	John 15:5	Deuteronomy 31:6
John 15:14	Psalm 108:13	Joshua 1:9

STRATEGY: I—INTREPID—BE INTREPID.

Summary: Do not fear. Don't be afraid. Have confidence in God and in His Word.

References:

Deuteronomy 20:1-4	Matthew 10:28	James 1:6
John 15:14	Luke 12:6-7	Romans 8:31
John 15:5	1 Corinthians 16:13	Psalm 27:1-3
Psalm 108:13	2 Timothy 1:7	Psalm 56:3
Deuteronomy 31:6	Acts 4:31	Isaiah 50:10
Joshua 1:9	Proverbs 28:1	Psalm 56:11
1 John 4:4	Exodus 14:14	Luke 17:5-10
Hebrews 13:5-6	Hebrews 11:6	Luke 12:4

KEY WORD: INTREPID

Key Verses: (fill in the blanks)

"For God has not given us the spirit of _____, but of power, and of love, and of a _____ mind" (2 Timothy 1:7).

"The Lord is my light and my salvation; whom shall I _____?

The Lord is the strength of my life; of whom should I be _____?

When the wicked came against me to eat up my flesh,

My enemies and foes, they stumbled and fell.

Though an army may encamp against me, my heart shall not _____;

Though war may rise against me, in this I will be _____."

(Psalm 27:1-3)

"Whenever I am afraid, I will _____ in You" (Psalm 56:3).

"What then shall we say to these things? If God is _____ us, who can be _____ us?" (Romans 8:31)

KEY TERMS:

Ahijah: Friend of God.

Intrepid: fearless, unafraid, undaunted, bold, daring, brave.

Faith: confidence

Forty: symbolizes testing, purifying, preparation, and cleansing

KEY POINT:

"Fear is spiritual, but it's not from God. He gives us power, love, and the ability to think. Satan knows that the best way to dumb people down is to scare them. And giants who want to control you don't use reason. They use fear."

THINK ABOUT IT—TALK ABOUT IT

I: Be _____

1. What are some synonyms for Intrepid?

2. Why is fear so dangerous?

3. Is fear a sin?

3. How many verses can you think of that tell us to not be afraid? Which is the most meaningful to you and why?

4. What frightens you?

5. What should you do when you begin to feel afraid?

6. What word is a synonym for faith?

7. How are fear and faith related?

8. Why is it important to have bold, Bible-teaching, spiritual leaders?

THE GOLIATH CODE
A BIBLICAL BATTLE PLAN
SESSION 5: AIM

HISTORY: SHIELD BUSTERS, PART 1, DISTRACTORS

Text: 1 Samuel 17:28-30

"Now Eliab his oldest brother heard when he spoke to the men; and Eliab's anger was aroused against David, and he said, 'Why did you come down here? And with whom have you left those few sheep in the wilderness? I know your pride and the insolence of your heart, for you have come down to see the battle.'

And David said, 'What have I done now? Is there not a cause?' Then he turned from him toward another and said the same thing; and these people answered him as the first ones did" (1 Samuel 17:28-30).

References:

Proverbs 14:17

Proverbs 29:11

Proverbs 15:1

Proverbs 29:9

Joshua 1:11

Joshua 24:14-15

Proverbs 4:25-27

Psalm 27:4

STRATEGY: A–AIM—AIM TO PLEASE GOD

Summary: Keep your focus on the mission and the Audience of One. Ignore distractions. Silence the distracting shield busters by answering their questions with questions.

_____

_____

_____

_____

_____

_____

_____

_____

_____

_____

References:

Proverbs 26:4-5	Colossians 4:5-6	Colossians 3:2
Proverbs 18:2	Matthew 10:36-39	1 Corinthians 10:31
Luke 20:23-24	John 12:26	Philippians 2:13-14
Luke 20:4	John 10:27	Hebrews 12:1-2
John 8:7	2 Timothy 2:4	Matthew 25:21
Luke 18:19	2 Corinthians 5:9	Matthew 6:33

KEY WORD: AIM

Key Verses: (fill in the blanks)

"Let your eyes look _____ ahead, and your eyelids look right before you. Ponder the path of your feet and let all your ways be established. Do not _____ to the right or the left; remove your foot from evil" (Proverbs 4:25-27).

"Therefore we make it our _____, whether present or absent, to be well pleasing to Him" (2 Corinthians 5:9).

"Set your mind on things _____, not on things on the _____" (Colossians 3:2).

"Brethren, I do not count myself to have apprehended; but _____ thing I do, forgetting those things which are behind and reaching forward to those things which are ahead, I press toward the _____ for the prize of the upward call of God in Christ Jesus" (Philippians 2:13-14).

KEY TERMS:

Shield Buster: Someone who tries to destroy your shield of faith, either wittingly or unwittingly.

Distractor: Someone who distracts.

Fool: Someone who acts contrary to God's Word because they don't know the Truth, and don't want to know it.

KEY POINT:

"One danger of a distraction is it causes you to forget who you really are, what your mission is, and what your vision looks like."

THINK ABOUT IT—TALK ABOUT IT

A: _____ To Please God

1. What is a shield buster, and why are they called that?

2. Have you ever known a distracting shield buster?

3. What are some distractions that affect you?

4. How can we keep from being distracted?

5. What is your "cause?"

6. How can you answer a fool without answering them?

_____

_____

_____

_____

7. Which verses regarding focusing are the most meaningful to you?

_____

_____

_____

_____

8. Why is answering a question with a question so effective when dealing with foolish shield busters?

_____

_____

_____

_____

THE GOLIATH CODE
A BIBLICAL BATTLE PLAN
SESSION 6: TRUTH

HISTORY: SHIELD BUSTERS, PART 2, DECEIVERS

Text: 1 Samuel 17:31-37

"Now when the words which David spoke were heard, they reported them to Saul; and he sent for him. Then David said to Saul, 'Let no man's heart fail because of him; your servant will go and fight with this Philistine.' And Saul said to David, 'You are not able to go against this Philistine to fight with him; for you are a youth, and he a man of war from his youth.'

But David said to Saul, 'Your servant used to keep his father's sheep, and when a lion or a bear came and took a lamb out of the flock, I went out after it and struck it, and delivered the lamb from its mouth; and when it arose against me, I caught it by its beard, and struck and killed it. Your servant has killed both lion and bear; and this uncircumcised Philistine will be like one of them, seeing he has defied the armies of the living God.' Moreover David said, 'The Lord, who delivered me from the paw of the lion and from the paw of the bear, He will deliver me from the hand of this Philistine.' And Saul said to David, 'Go, and the Lord be with you!'" (1 Samuel 17:31-37).

References:

1 Samuel 8:10-20
1 Samuel 9:2

STRATEGY: TRUTH—SPEAK THE TRUTH

Summary: Counter the lies told by the deceiving shield busters with the truth of God's Word and your own testimony.

References:

Philippians 4:13	Philippians 1:6	Psalm 119:11
1 Corinthians 10:23	Proverbs 24:16	Psalm 77:11-12
Proverbs 20:1	Romans 14:13	Psalm 105:1-6
John 1:17	John 8:31-32	

KEY WORD: TRUTH

Key Verses: (fill in the blanks)

"For the law was given through Moses, but grace and _____ came through Jesus Christ" (John 1:17).

"Being _____ of this very thing, that He who began a good _____ in you will be faithful to _____ it until the day of Jesus Christ" (Philippians 1:6).

"If you abide in My _____, you are My disciples indeed. And you shall know the truth, and the truth shall make you _____" (John 8:31-32).

"I will remember the _____ of the Lord; Surely I will remember Your wonders of old. I will also meditate on all Your work, and talk of Your _____" (Psalm 77:11-12).

KEY TERMS:

Saul: Demanding

Shield Buster: Someone who tries to destroy your shield of faith, either wittingly or unwittingly.

Deceiver: Someone who deceives, whether intentionally or not.

Scoffer: Someone who acts contrary to God's Word, even though they know it. AKA: Mocker.

Truth: That which corresponds to reality; God's Word; Jesus

Testimony: A personal proclamation given by a witness as evidence of the truth.

KEY POINT:

"The late Dr. Adrian Rogers once said, 'A Christian with a testimony is never at the mercy of an unbeliever with an argument.'"

THINK ABOUT IT—TALK ABOUT IT

T: Speak the _____

1. Have you ever had to confront a deceiver?

2. Are shield busters our enemies?

3. What are some deceptions that have affected you?

4. What is truth?

5. Why is your testimony so powerful when dealing with shield busters?

6. List some things God has done for you.

_____

_____

_____

_____

7. Grace without truth is _____.

_____

_____

_____

_____

8. Truth without grace is _____.

_____

_____

_____

_____

9. Truth with grace is _____.

_____

_____

_____

_____

THE GOLIATH CODE
A BIBLICAL BATTLE PLAN
SESSION 7: HARDWARE

HISTORY: THE WEAPONS

Text: Samuel 17:38-40

"So Saul clothed David with his armor, and he put a bronze helmet on his head; he also clothed him with a coat of mail. David fastened his sword to his armor and tried to walk, for he had not tested them. And David said to Saul, 'I cannot walk with these, for I have not tested them.' So David took them off. Then he took his staff in his hand; and he chose for himself five smooth stones from the brook, and put them in a shepherd's bag, in a pouch which he had, and his sling was in his hand. And he drew near to the Philistine" (1 Samuel 17:38-40).

_____

_____

_____

_____

_____

_____

_____

_____

_____

_____

References:

1 Samuel 16:18

STRATEGY: H—HARDWARE—USE THE RIGHT HARDWARE

Summary: Put on the whole armor of God, every day. Only spiritual armor is completely effective in spiritual warfare, and all our battles are spiritual.

Jesus Christ is the Armor of God.

References:

2 Corinthians 10:3-5

Ephesians 6:10-13

Ephesians 6:14-18

Ephesians 4:25

Colossians 3:9

Colossians 3:5-8

Colossians 3:12

Romans 12:18

Colossians 3:15

Hebrews 11:6

Colossians 3:17

Ephesians 5:20

Colossians 3:2

Ephesians 4:23

Romans 12:2

Hebrews 4:12

1 Corinthians 2:4-5

Psalm 119:105

Colossians 4:2

Philippians 4:6

Luke 11:9

Isaiah 30:21

Jeremiah 33:3

Psalm 50:15

James 5:16b

Galatians 3:27

Romans 13:12 & 14

John 14:6

Jeremiah 23:6

1 Corinthians 1:30

Ephesians 2:14

John 14:27

Romans 16:20

Psalm 119:114

Psalm 18:2

Psalm 65:5

Isaiah 12:2

Psalm 27:1

John 1:1

John 1:14

Revelation 19:13

Ephesians 2:18

Romans 8:34

John 16:23

KEY WORD: HARDWARE

Key Verses: (fill in the blanks)

"For though we walk in the flesh, we do not war according to the _____. For the weapons of our warfare are not _____ but mighty in God for pulling down strongholds, casting down arguments and every high thing that exalts itself against the knowledge of God, bringing every thought into captivity to the obedience of Christ" (2 Corinthians 10:3-5).

"Finally, my brethren, be strong ____ ____ _____ and in the power of His might. Put on the whole _____ of God, that you may be able to stand against the wiles of the devil" (Ephesians 6:10-11).

"But _____ _____ the Lord Jesus, and make no provision for the flesh, to fulfill its lusts" (Romans 13:14)

"For as many of you as were baptized _____ Christ have _____ ____ Christ" (Galatians 3:27).

KEY TERMS:

Hardware: Equipment designed for a particular purpose.

Armor: A strong outer covering worn for protection, especially in battle.

KEY POINT:

"Why would we ever want to use inferior weapons (even if they are the best the world has to offer), instead of the mighty spiritual weapons God has provided us?"

THINK ABOUT IT—TALK ABOUT IT

H: Use the Right _____

1. Why couldn't David use Saul's armor?

   _____

   _____

   _____

   _____

2. What is the belt of truth?

   _____

   _____

   _____

   _____

3. How is the breastplate of righteousness like "right-choice-ness?"

   _____

   _____

   _____

   _____

4. Peace is not the _____ of conflict. It is the _____ of God.

   _____

   _____

   _____

5. How is being thankful an expression of faith?

   _____

   _____

   _____

   _____

6. What does the helmet protect?

7. Why is the Word called the sword of the Spirit?

8. How is the walkie-talkie different from a cell phone?

9. How does it help to realize that Jesus *is* the Armor of God?

THE GOLIATH CODE
A BIBLICAL BATTLE PLAN
SESSION 8: CONFESS

HISTORY: OPENING SALVO

Text: 1 Samuel 17:41-47

"So the Philistine came, and began drawing near to David, and the man who bore the shield went before him. And when the Philistine looked about and saw David, he disdained him; for he was only a youth, ruddy and good-looking. So the Philistine said to David, 'Am I a dog, that you come to me with sticks?' And the Philistine cursed David by his gods. And the Philistine said to David, 'Come to me, and I will give your flesh to the birds of the air and the beasts of the field!'

"Then David said to the Philistine, 'You come to me with a sword, with a spear, and with a javelin. But I come to you in the name of the LORD of hosts, the God of the armies of Israel, whom you have defied.

'This day the LORD will deliver you into my hand, and I will strike you and take your head from you. And this day I will give the carcasses of the camp of the Philistines to the birds of the air and the wild beasts of the earth, that all the earth may know that there is a God in Israel. Then all this assembly shall know that the LORD does not save with sword and spear; for the battle is the LORD's, and He will give you into our hands'" (1 Samuel 17:41-47).

_____

_____

_____

References:

1 Corinthians 10:20	Romans 3:14	Proverbs 26:2
Genesis 12:3	Psalm 1:4-6	1 Samuel 17:45
Psalm 10:7	Proverbs 11:31	Isaiah 54:15-17

STRATEGY: C-CONFESS—CONFESS THE LORD

Summary: Speak the Word. Call out Jesus' name. If you belong to God, say so. Say it aloud. Use the authority you have as a Child of the King. Speak directly to the giant and ignore the shield bearer.

Don't waste time telling God how big the giants are. Tell the giants how big your God is.

References:

Psalm 20:7

Proverbs 18:10

Proverbs 18:21

Matthew 12:36-37

Romans 10:9-10

Romans 10:13

Luke 12:8

Psalm 107:2

Matthew 21:21

Luke 10:19

Luke 10:16

2 Corinthians 1:4

Psalm 50:15

Romans 8:37

Psalm 56:9

Romans 8:31

KEY WORD: CONFESS

Key Verses: (fill in the blanks)

"You come to me with a sword, with a spear, and with a javelin. But I come to you in the _____ of the LORD of _____, the God of the armies of Israel, whom you have defied" (1 Samuel 17:45).

"No _____ formed against you shall prosper, and every _____ which rises against you in judgment you shall condemn. This is the heritage of the servants of the Lord, and their _____ is from Me,' says the Lord." (Isaiah 54:17).

"Life and death are in the power of the _____" (Proverbs 18:21).

"Behold I give you the _____ to trample on serpents and scorpions, and over all the power of the enemy, and nothing shall by any means hurt you" (Luke 10:19)

"Let the redeemed of the LORD _____ ____, whom He has redeemed from the hand of the enemy" (Psalm 107:2).

KEY TERMS:

Confess: Declare out loud. In this context, the same as "profess". Literally: "to say the same as".

Lord of Hosts: Commander-in-Chief of the armies of heaven.

KEY POINT:

"Remember, the battle is the Lord's—not ours. Even so, we have our jobs to do, in His strength, as His servants. One of those jobs is to exercise our authority and confess Him out loud so the adversary can hear it."

THINK ABOUT IT—TALK ABOUT IT

C: _____ the Lord

1. Are pagan gods real?

2. Should we be concerned about pagan curses?

3. What does it mean to confess the Lord?

4. Why is it important to confess the Lord with your mouth?

5. How should we fight the shield bearers?

6. What should you say to a giant?

    _____

    _____

    _____

    _____

7. How does the enemy defy the Lord when he comes against us?

    _____

    _____

    _____

    _____

8. According to verse 47, what were God's people to learn from Goliath's defeat?

    _____

    _____

    _____

    _____

THE GOLIATH CODE
A BIBLICAL BATTLE PLAN
SESSION 9: OVERCOME

HISTORY: THE ATTACK

Text: 1 Samuel 17:48-50

"So it was, when the Philistine arose and came and drew near to meet David, that David hurried and ran toward the army to meet the Philistine. Then David put his hand in his bag and took out a stone; and he slung it and struck the Philistine in his forehead, so that the stone sank into his forehead, and he fell on his face to the earth. So David prevailed over the Philistine with a sling and a stone, and struck the Philistine and killed him" (1 Samuel 17:48-50).

References:

Psalm 86:3
1 Thessalonians 5:17

STRATEGY: O—OVERCOME—OVERCOME!

Summary: If you are in Christ, you're an overcomer. Learn when to charge, stand your ground, or retreat.

_____

_____

_____

_____

_____

_____

_____

_____

_____

_____

_____

References:

1 John 5:5	Ephesians 6:13-14	Psalm 31:3
James 4:7	1 Corinthians 6:18	Psalm 108:1
1 Peter 5:9	1 Timothy 6:11	Psalm 1:3
Psalm 119:32	2 Timothy 2:22	Psalm 108:10-11a
Matthew 28:19	1 Corinthians 10:13	Psalm 109:23
Philippians 3:12-14	Isaiah 40:31	Matthew 16:15-19
Ephesians 6:11	Romans 11:29	Zechariah 4:6

KEY WORD: OVERCOME

Key Verses: (fill in the blanks)

"Who is he who overcomes the world, but he who _____ that Jesus is the Son of God?" (1 John 5:5).

"Therefore submit to God. _____ the devil and he will flee from you" (James 4:7).

"Therefore take up the whole armor of God, that you may be able to _____ in the evil day, and having done all, to _____" (Ephesians 6:13).

"But you, O man of God, _____ these things and pursue righteousness, godliness, faith, love, patience, gentleness" (1 Timothy 6:11).

"This is the word of the Lord to Zerubbabel: 'Not by might nor by power, but by My _____,' says the Lord of hosts" (Zechariah 4:6).

KEY TERMS:

Overcome: Overpower. Overwhelm. Conquer. Surmount. Rise above. Be victorious.

Petros: A small stone. The Greek name "Peter".

KEY POINT:

"How can we know when to stand, retreat, or charge? The answer depends on where you are, versus where you are supposed to be."

THINK ABOUT IT—TALK ABOUT IT

O: _____!

1. Who is an "Overcomer"?

2. When should we charge (run) to the battle?

3. Describe a time when you were supposed to charge.

4. When should we stay put (stand our ground)?

5. Describe a time when you were supposed to stand firm?

6. When should we retreat (bug out)?

_____

_____

_____

_____

7. Describe a time when you were supposed to retreat?

_____

_____

_____

_____

8. Where should we run to when we charge or retreat?

_____

_____

_____

_____

9. What does it mean to "overcome"?

_____

_____

_____

_____

THE GOLIATH CODE
A BIBLICAL BATTLE PLAN
SESSION 10: DEMONSTRATE

HISTORY: THE COUP DE GRÂCE

Text: 1 Samuel 17:50-54

"But there was no sword in the hand of David. Therefore David ran and stood over the Philistine, took his sword and drew it out of its sheath and killed him, and cut off his head with it. And when the Philistines saw that their champion was dead, they fled. Now the men of Israel and Judah arose and shouted, and pursued the Philistines as far as the entrance of the valley and to the gates of Ekron. And the wounded of the Philistines fell along the road to Shaaraim, even as far as Gath and Ekron.

Then the children of Israel returned from chasing the Philistines, and they plundered their tents. And David took the head of the Philistine and brought it to Jerusalem, but he put his armor in his tent" (1 Samuel 17:50-54).

References:

1 Samuel 21:9   John 16:33

1 Corinthians 15:57   Luke 21:24

STRATEGY: D—DEMONSTRATE—DEMONSTRATE YOUR FAITH

Summary: Discourage the enemy and encourage the family of God by showing them your faith by your works.

_____

_____

_____

_____

_____

_____

_____

_____

_____

_____

_____

References:

Ephesians 6:12	Galatians 2:20	
John 10:10	1 Corinthians 6:18	Acts 14:22
Hebrews 11:32-34	John 8:36	1 Peter 5:3
1 John 5:4	2 Corinthians 5:17	1 Timothy 4:12
James 2:18	Hebrews 10:24-25	Matthew 5:16
Colossians 3:3	Hebrews 3:13	

KEY WORD: DEMONSTRATE

Key Verses: (fill in the blanks)

"For whatever is born of God _____ the world. And this is the victory that has overcome the world—our _____" (1 John 5:4).

"Show me your faith without your _____, and I will _____ you my faith by my works" (James 2:18).

"But _____ one another daily, while it is called 'Today,' lest any of you be hardened through the deceitfulness of sin" (Hebrews 3:13).

"Let your light so shine before men, that they may see your _____ _____ and glorify your Father in heaven" (Matthew 5:16).

KEY TERMS:

Killed (v50): וַהֲמִיתֵמְיָו *Uimetheu.* Put to death.

Yod: י Hebrew letter meaning hand, might or power.

Tav: ת Hebrew letter meaning mark or seal.

Killed (v51): וַהֲמִיתֵמְיָו *Uimttheu.* Marked or sealed in death.

Champion *(v51):* *Gibbor.* Powerful bully or tyrant.

Shaaraim: Double gates.

Ekron: Extinction.

Salem: Shalom. Peace.

Jebus: Trample, thresh, or downtrodden.

Gol: Skull

Jerusalem: *Yireh-Shalem.* He will provide peace.

KEY POINT:

"We cannot be satisfied with quietly killing one giant and then going back to keeping sheep in obscurity. Complete victory requires us to run and stand over the dead giant and make sure everyone around us knows it is dead."

THINK ABOUT IT—TALK ABOUT IT

D: _____ Your Faith

1. What killed the giant?

2. Why did David cut off the giant's head?

3. What are some ways you can demonstrate your faith?

4. Why is it important to show your faith?

5. Who benefits when we demonstrate our faith?

6. How does demonstrating our faith encourage other believers?

_____

_____

_____

_____

7. How does demonstrating our faith discourage the forces of darkness?

_____

_____

_____

_____

8. What things become new when you become a Christian?

_____

_____

_____

_____

THE GOLIATH CODE
A BIBLICAL BATTLE PLAN
SESSION 11: ENDURE

HISTORY: POST-BATTLE DEBRIEFING

Text:1 Samuel 17:55-58

"When Saul saw David going out against the Philistine, he said to Abner, 'Abner, whose son is this youth?' And Abner said, 'As your soul lives, O king, I do not know.' So the king said, 'Inquire whose son this young man is.' Then, as David returned from the slaughter of the Philistine, Abner took him before Saul with the head of the Philistine in his hand. And Saul said to him, 'Whose son are you, young man?' So David answered, "I am the son of your servant Jesse the Bethlehemite'" (1 Samuel 17:55-58).

References:

1 Samuel 16:21-23	1 Corinthians 2:14	
1 Samuel 17:12	James 3:16	Jude 1:19
Romans 8:16	James 1:17	

STRATEGY: E—ENDURE—ENDURE TO THE END

Summary: Memorable battles come and go but keep your armor on until you hear the Lord say, "Come up here!" Practice faith, hope, and love with joy. Never, ever, give up.

We are not home yet, but I've read the end of the Book—we win!

References:

1 Peter 5:8

2 Timothy 4:5

2 Timothy 3:12

2 Timothy 2:3

Hebrews 10:32-35

James 1:12

James 5:10-11

Hebrews 12:1

Hebrews 12:7

2 Timothy 2:10

James 5:7

1 Corinthians 10:31

Ephesians 6:11, 13, 14

Hebrews 10:35-36

1 Thessalonians 5:16-18

Hebrews 12:1-3

John 16:33

1 Peter 2:21

Acts 24:15

Psalm 31:24

Psalm 42:11

Psalm 130:5

Romans 8:25

1 Thessalonians 5:8

1 Corinthians 16:13-14

Matthew 5:44

James 1:2

Philippians 4:4

Nehemiah 8:10

Psalm 30:4-5

2 Corinthians 12:9-10

KEY WORD: ENDURE

Key Verses: (fill in the blanks)

"Where _____ and self-seeking exist, _____ and every evil thing are there" (James 3:16).

"Be sober, be vigilant; because your adversary the _____ walks about like a roaring lion, seeking whom he may _____" (1 Peter 5:8).

"Therefore we also, since we are _____ by so great a cloud of witnesses, let us lay aside every weight, and the sin which so easily ensnares us, and let us run with _____ the race that is set before us" (Hebrews 12:1).

"Therefore do not cast away your confidence, which has great reward. For you have need of _____, so that after you have done the will of God, you may receive the promise" (Hebrews 10:35-36).

KEY TERMS:

Jesse: Existing.

Ephrathite: Fruitful.

Abner: Father of Light.

Chesed: Grace, mercy, love, or loving kindness.

Rejoice: Refill your Joy tank.

KEY POINT:

"Most of our time is not spent fighting big, exciting battles, but in working, waiting, and walking through this evil and fallen world. That is why the Bible is replete with commands for us to endure, stand firm, and persevere; as well as those that tell us to be steadfast, immovable, vigilant, patient, long-suffering, and strong."

THINK ABOUT IT—TALK ABOUT IT

E: _____ to the End

1. Why is the phrase, "all men are created equal" incompatible with paganism and evolution?

    _____

    _____

    _____

    _____

2. Why were Saul and Abner not encouraged by David's victory?

    _____

    _____

    _____

    _____

3. Why do we tend to take our armor off after a victory?

    _____

    _____

    _____

    _____

4. List some things we must endure:

    _____

    _____

    _____

    _____

5. What do we gain by endurance?

    _____

    _____

    _____

    _____

6. What are some of the traits of the Lord which will endure forever?

_____

_____

_____

_____

7. How can you endure?

    a. Keep your _____ on.

    b. Keep your _____ right. Spiritual endurance requires _____, _____, _____, and _____.

    c. Keep your eyes on _____.

8. To "rejoice" means to _____ your _____ tank.

_____

_____

_____

_____

EPILOGUE
THE GOLIATH CODE

David's victory vividly illustrates how we too can conquer our giants. I created the mnemonic "GOLIATH CODE" to help you remember and apply David's story to yours.

Whenever you face a giant, remember:

G: Geography—Understand the Geography. Your enemy is wedged between a hedge and a fence and can never cross the boundary of the blood. You, on the other hand, are in Christ the Ram—the position of strength.

O: Opponent—Recognize your Opponent. Learn to recognize spiritual giants and the bondage they bring. Don't waste your time or ammunition fighting the shield bearers.

L: Labels—Use the Right Labels. Never accept the labels Satan or the world tries to stick on you. You are who God says you are, not what you do.

I: Intrepid—Be Intrepid. Do not fear. Don't be afraid. Have confidence in God and in His Word.

A: Aim—Aim to Please God. Keep your focus on the mission and the Audience of One. Ignore distractions. Silence the distracting shield busters by answering their questions with questions.

T: Truth—Speak the Truth. Counter the lies told by the deceiving shield busters with the truth of God's Word and your own testimony.

H: Hardware—Use the Right Hardware. Put on the whole armor of God, every day. Only spiritual armor is completely effective in spiritual warfare. And all our battles are spiritual.

C: Confess—Confess the Lord. Speak the Word. Call out Jesus' name. If you belong to God, say so. Say it aloud. Use the authority you have as a Child of the King. Don't waste time telling God how big the giants are. Tell the giants how big your God is.

O: Overcome—Overcome! If you are in Christ, you are an overcomer. Learn when to charge, stand your ground, or retreat.

D: Demonstrate—Demonstrate your Faith. Discourage the enemy and encourage the family of God by showing them your faith by your works.

E: Endure—Endure to the End. Memorable battles come and go, but keep your armor on until you hear the Lord say, "Come up here!" Practice faith, hope, and love with joy. We are not home yet, but I've read the end of the Book—we win!

THE GOLIATH CODE

Fill in the blanks with the key words:

G: Understand the _____

O: Recognize Your _____

L: Use the Right _____

I: Be _____

A: _____ to Please God

T: Speak the _____

H: Use the Right _____

C: _____ the Lord

O: _____!

D: _____ Your Faith

E: _____ to the End

THINK ABOUT IT—TALK ABOUT IT

1. What is the most significant thing you have learned from this study?

_____

_____

_____

_____

2. What spiritual battle are you facing that you can use this strategy to fight?

_____

_____

_____

_____

LABELS THAT GOD GIVES US
(WHO WE ARE IN CHRIST)

- "A Holy Nation" (1 Peter 2:9)
- "A Royal Priesthood" (1 Peter 2:9)
- "Able To Do All Things Through Christ" (Philippians 4:13)
- "Abraham's Seed" (Galatians 3:29)
- "Accepted in the Beloved" (Ephesians 1:6)
- "Adopted" (Romans 8:15)
- "Alive Together with Him" (Colossians 2:13)
- "Already Clean" (John 15:3)
- "Ambassadors for Christ" (2 Corinthians 5:20)
- "Appointed to Affliction" (1 Thessalonians 3:3)
- "Authorized" (Luke 10:19)
- "Baptized By One Spirit into One Body" (1 Corinthians 12:13)
- "Becoming the Righteousness of God" (2 Corinthians 5:21)
- "Being Transformed into His Image from Glory to Glory" (2 Corinthians 3:18)
- "Believers" (Acts 5:14)
- "Beloved of God" (Romans 1:7; Colossians 3:12)
- "Blameless" (Colossians 1:22; 1 Corinthians 1:8; 1 Thessalonians 5:23; Psalm 37:37; Proverbs 2:21; 11:5; Philippians 3:6; Luke 1:6)
- "Blessed With Every Spiritual Blessing" (Ephesians 1:3)
- "Born Again" (1 Peter 1:23)
- "Born of God" (1 John 5:1)
- "Bought at a Price" (1 Corinthians 6:20)
- "Bound To Thank God Always" (2 Thessalonians 1:3; 2:13)
- "Brethren" (Matthew 23:8)
- "Called" (2 Thessalonians 2:14)
- "Called by His Name" (Acts 15:17)
- "Called Into the Fellowship of His Son" (1 Corinthians 1:9)
- "Children of God" (John 1:12; 1 John 3:1)
- "Children of the Promise" (Galatians 4:28)
- "Chosen" (Revelation 17:14)
- "Chosen Generation" (1 Peter 2:9)
- "Christ's" (1 Corinthians 3:23)
- "Clay in the Potter's Hand" (Isaiah 64:8)
- "Clean" (John 13:10)
- "Complete" (Colossians 2:10)
- "Created in Christ Jesus for Good Works" (Ephesians 2:10)
- "Crucified with Christ" (Galatians 2:20)
- "Debtors, but Not to the Flesh" (Romans 8:12)
- "Delivered from the Power of Darkness" (Colossians 1:13)

- "Dependent on the Lord" (Isaiah 10:20)
- "Dwelling Place of God in the Spirit" (Ephesians 2:22)
- "Empowered" (2 Timothy 1:7)
- "Epistles of Christ" (2 Corinthians 3:3)
- "Escaped From the Corruption That is in the World" (2 Peter 1:4)
- "Family" (Ephesians 3:15)
- "Followers of the Lord" (1 Thessalonians 1:6)
- "Forgiven of all My Trespasses" (Colossians 2:13)
- "Free Indeed" (John 8:36)
- "Gifted" (Romans 12:6)
- "God's Building" (1 Corinthians 3:9)
- "God's Fellow Workers" (1 Corinthians 3:9)
- "God's Field" (1 Corinthians 3:9)
- "Granted To Suffer" (Philippians 1:29)
- "Hard-Pressed On Every Side, Yet Not Crushed" (2 Corinthians 4:8)
- "Healed" (Isaiah 53:5)
- "Heirs According to the Promise" (Galatians 3:29)
- "Heirs of God" (Romans 8:17)
- "His Disciples" (John 8:31; 13:35)
- "His Friends" (John 15:14)
- "His Own" (John 13:1)
- "His Own Special People" (1 Peter 2:9)
- "His People" (Psalm 100:3)
- "His Sheep" (John 10:27)
- "His Workmanship" (Ephesians 2:10)
- "Holy" (1 Corinthians 3:16-17; Colossians 3:12)
- "In Christ Jesus" (1 Corinthians 1:30)
- "In God" (Colossians 3:3)
- "In Him Who is True" (1 John 5:20)
- "Indwelt" (Romans 8:11)
- "Joint Heirs with Christ" (Romans 8:17)
- "Just" (Hebrews 10:38)
- "Justified" (1 Corinthians 6:11)
- "Kings" (Revelation 1:6)
- "Light In the Lord" (Ephesians 5:8)
- "Little Children" (1 John 2:1; Galatians 4:19)
- "Living Stones" (1 Peter 2:5)
- "Loved" (1 John 4:10)
- "Loved by God" (Galatians 2:20)
- "Members of His Body" (Ephesians 5:30)
- "Members of One Another" (Ephesians 4:25)
- "Members of the Household of God" (Ephesians 2:19)
- "Ministers of the New Covenant" (2 Corinthians 3:6)
- "More Than Conquerors Through Him" (Romans 8:37)
- "New Creations" (2 Corinthians 5:17)
- "New Lumps" (1 Corinthians 5:7)
- "No Longer Slaves" (Galatians 4:7)

- "No Longer Strangers and Foreigners, but Fellow Citizens with the Saints" (Ephesians 2:19)
- "Not in the Flesh but in the Spirit" (Romans 8:9)
- "Not of the World" (John 15:19)
- "Not Our Own" (1 Corinthians 6:19)
- "Not Under Law but Under Grace" (Romans 6:14; Galatians 5:18)
- "Of God" (1 John 5:19)
- "Of the Truth" (1 John 3:19)
- "Of Those Who Believe" (Hebrews 10:39)
- "One in Christ Jesus" (Galatians 3:28)
- "Overcomers" (1 John 4:4)
- "Partakers of Christ" (Hebrews 3:14)
- "Partakers of Grace" (Philippians 1:7)
- "Partakers of His Promise in Christ" (Ephesians 3:6)
- "Partakers of the Heavenly Calling" (Hebrews 3:1)
- "Partakers of the Holy Spirit" (Hebrews 6:4)
- "Partakers of the Inheritance of the Saints in the Light" (Colossians 1:12)
- "Partakers of the Sufferings (of Christ)" (2 Corinthians 1:7)
- "Perplexed, but Not in Despair" (2 Corinthians 4:8)
- "Persecuted, but Not Forsaken" (2 Corinthians 4:9)
- "Precious" (Isaiah 43:4)

- "Predestined to be Conformed to the Image of His Son" (Romans 8:29)
- "Priests" (Revelation 1:6)
- "Receiving A Kingdom Which Cannot Be Shaken" (Hebrews 12:28)
- "Reconciled" (Colossians 1:21)
- "Redeemed" (Galatians 4:5; Psalm 107:2)
- "Righteous" (Romans 5:19; 9:30; 1 Peter 3:12; Philippians 3:9; Psalm 1:6; 32:11; 37:19 & 39; Luke 1:6)
- "Safe" (Proverbs 18:10)
- "Saints" (Romans 1:7)
- "Sanctified" (1 Corinthians 6:11)
- "Saved" (1 Corinthians 15:2)
- "Saved by Grace" (Ephesians 2:8)
- "Sealed" (2 Corinthians 1:22; Ephesians 1:13; 4:30)
- "Servants of Christ" (1 Corinthians 4:1)
- "Serving the Lord Christ" (Colossians 3:24)
- "Set Free from Sin" (Romans 6:18)
- "Slaves of God" (Romans 6:22)
- "Slaves of Righteousness" (Romans 6:18)
- "Soldiers of Jesus Christ" (2 Timothy 2:3)
- "Sons of God" (Galatians 3:26; Galatians 4:6)
- "Sons of Light" (1 Thessalonians 5:5)
- "Sons of the Day" (1 Thessalonians 5:5)
- "Stewards of the Mysteries of God" (1 Corinthians 4:1)

- "Struck Down, but Not Destroyed" (2 Corinthians 4:9)
- "Subject To Christ" (Ephesians 5:24)
- "Sufficient" (With Our Sufficiency from God) (2 Corinthians 3:5)
- "Surrounded By a Great Cloud of Witnesses" (Hebrews 12:1)
- "The Apple of His Eye" (Zechariah 2:8)
- "The Body of Christ" (1 Corinthians 12:27)
- "The Branches" (John 15:5)
- "The Elect of God" (Colossians 3:12)
- "The Fragrance of Christ" (2 Corinthians 2:15)
- "The Light of the World" (Matthew 5:14)
- "The Lord's" (Romans 14:8)
- "The People of His Pasture" (Psalm 95:7)
- "The Salt of the Earth" (Matthew 5:13)
- "The Sheep of His Hand" (Psalm 95:7)
- "The Sheep of His Pasture" (Psalm 100:3)
- "The Temple of God" (1 Corinthians 3:16)
- "The Temple of the Holy Spirit" (1 Corinthians 6:19)
- "The Work of His Hand" (Isaiah 64:8)
- "Triumphant" (2 Corinthians 2:14)
- "Truly Unleavened" (1 Corinthians 5:7)
- "Unable to Do Anything Without Him" (John 15:5)
- "Upright" (Psalm 32:11; 37:18; Proverbs 2:21; 29:10)
- "Valuable" (Matthew 10:31; Luke 12:7)
- "Victorious" (1 Corinthians 15:57)
- "Washed" (1 Corinthians 6:11)
- "Witnesses" (1 Thessalonians 2:10)

HOW TO BECOME A NEW CREATION
THE ABCS OF SALVATION

What must you do to become a new creation and receive eternal life? It's as simple as ABC...

<u>A</u>dmit you are a sinner.

"For all have sinned and fall short of the glory of God" (Romans 3:23).

You cannot be good enough or do well enough to earn your way into God's perfect heaven.

"For the wages of sin is death, but the gift of God is eternal life in Christ Jesus our Lord" (Romans 6:23).

We have all earned the judgment of eternal death, which is separation from God, but God offers us the gift of eternal life "in Christ." It is free to us, but Jesus paid for it with His own blood. He earned the title "Lord".

<u>B</u>elieve Jesus is who He says He is.

"For God so loved the world that He gave his only begotten Son, that whoever believes in Him should not perish, but have everlasting life" (John 3:16).

Jesus is God's first-born Son. If you believe in Him, you'll not suffer the wages of sin and *will* have life forever.

"Most assuredly I say to you, he who believes in Me has everlasting life" (John 6:47).

To "believe in" Him means to put all your trust in Him. Trust Him with your life.

You can be sure that the moment you believe in Him, you have everlasting life. You don't have to wait until death to receive it.

<u>C</u>onfess Jesus as your Lord.

"That if you confess with your mouth the Lord Jesus, and believe in your heart that God has raised Him from the dead, you will be saved. For with the heart one believes unto righteousness, and with the mouth confession is made unto salvation" (Romans 10:9-10).

This is not confessing your sin. You already did that when you admitted it. To confess something with your mouth is to say it aloud. "Lord" means owner (as in landlord), boss, or master. Rather than your lord being you, say that Jesus is your Lord.

Jesus' resurrection proved that the sacrifice of His sinless life was accepted by God as the complete payment for all our sin debt.

> "Therefore whoever confesses Me before men, him I will also confess before My Father in heaven. But whoever denies Me before men, him I will also deny before My Father who is in heaven" (Matthew 10:32-33).

When you tell others about Jesus, He tells God the Father about you!

> "For whoever calls on the name of the Lord shall be saved" (Romans 10:13).

Good news! No matter who you are or what you've done, once you call on Jesus' name as explained above, you become a new creation and the gift of eternal life is yours. God's Holy Spirit places you "in Christ" and actually sets up residence in you.

God no longer labels you as "ungodly" or "sinner." He says you are "righteous" and a "saint." Now go act like it!